GOOD FOR YOU!

A Tale of Love Woven in Poetry

PRINCESTAR

BookLeaf Publishing

India | USA | UK

Made with ❤ on the BookLeaf Publishing Platform

www.bookleafpub.in

www.bookleafpub.com

Dedication

To the ones who dare to love like fire — Burning bright, untamed, and unapologetic.

To those who refuse to settle for anything less than passion, chaos, and the raw truth of emotions.

To my fans, my believers, my people — this book is yours as much as it is mine.

This book is for you, for me, for every soul that knows love isn't just a feeling — it's a life force.

-PRINCESTAR

Preface

Love isn't a soft whisper. It's a passionate roar.

It's an unstoppable wave that crashes through life,
reshaping everything in its path.

This book isn't just poetry; it's a journey through love in
all its shades. Its highs, its lows, its madness, and its
magic.

These words are the truth of an artist who has lived,
loved, and conquered.

If you're here, you're ready to experience love the way I
do — bold, intense, and unforgettable.

-PRINCESTAR

Acknowledgements

To love itself — my greatest muse, my fiercest teacher.

To every heart that has touched mine, whether in passion or pain — you've given me stories to tell, and for that, I am grateful.

And to PRINCESTAR — the artist, the visionary, the force — I acknowledge myself because I built this. I lived this. And now, I give it to the world of mine.

-PRINCESTAR

1. CHEMICAL BOND

I want a Chemical Bond with you
Writing a fresh new song with you
Driving a beautiful super car with you
I want a Chemical Bond with you

I want to jump really high with you
I want to touch the sky with you
I want to feel the light with you
Flying like a beautiful kite with you

I want a Chemical Bond with you
Writing a fresh new song with you
Driving a beautiful super car with you
I want a Chemical Bond with you

I feel like being in spotlight with you
It feels super duper right with you
I want to take life's bite with you
On the bed of nature under the skies with you

I want a Chemical Bond with you
Writing a fresh new song with you
Driving a beautiful super car with you
I want a Chemical Bond with you

2. ALL IN ONE

Your fingers feel like a poetry on my skin
Your presence feels like I every day do win
Your words are an invisible energy flowing through my
spine
The battle in which ordinary people do take time

Your touch, a symphony, paints my canvas of desire,
Igniting flames within, like a passion of fire
Each stroke of your fingertips, a tender caress
Leaving trails of longing, my senses undress

Your voice, a whispered melody, echoes in my soul
A harmony of seduction that leaves me whole
Every word you speak, a spellbinding spell
Drawing me closer, under your enchanting spell

In your presence, I'm intoxicated, in a state of bliss
A dance of bodies, entwined in pure abyss
Ordinary moments become extraordinary scenes
As we transcend the mundane, exploring what love
exactly means

Your fingers, your words, your presence a divine
Weave a tapestry of passion on the line
Of an eternal dance, our hearts intertwined
Definition of us? Passion, love, and pleasure all in one
combined

3. BUMBLE

I saw you on Bumble
Your simplicity made my words fumble
Anyway, this world's a royal rumble
So, why not we together pick up our favourite dumbbell?

Please excuse me; I am not really humble
Yet I do stumble
Because of your beauty
In front of you, I do mumble!

Of course you are a whole package, a bundle
Of spice and sweetness, no grumble
You know what? This world is a messy jungle
And I found you, who will never let my heart crumble!

4. HAPPY TO BE THE REASON OF YOUR SMILE

I'm happy to be the reason of your smile
For more than a while
If, I'm already in your gallery's "favourites" file
Then, why don't you let me sing for you, in front of you,
when me meet on our next mile?

I'm happy to be the reason of your smile
You know that's my kinda style
I don't know why? but,
Whenever I do see you my words do a freestyle

There might be something about you, your eyes or your
hairstyle
Maybe, I will figure out when we meet on our next mile
But, I'm happy to be the reason of your smile
For more than a while

5. UNSEALED

If you are willing to believe in something unreal
I want you to break and unseal
The glass of a normal world, which has grown grey and
teal
In which you'll have me making you feel
All the rainbows and unicorns are real

Isn't that the world's most beautiful deal?
To experience this huge ride and feel
About everything existing and non existing
Like it's trapped in a world of reel.

It is a lavish wheel.
Like every craving, a heart's meal
It's just one word, love!
And all the fantasy in the real world is unsealed

6. THE TEMPLE OF DESIRE

Your body, the temple of desire,
A place where I find my heart's choir
Your curves and contours, a work of art,
That sets my soul and senses apart

Your skin, so soft so smooth to touch,
Arousing my senses, asking for much
I want to taste the nectar of love,
And dive into alluring sea of love

Your scent, a fragrance of love and lust,
That drives me crazy with a dizzy thirst
I want to explore every inch of you,
Drowning in the passion of pink and blue

Your lips, a promise of a sweet delight,
A kiss that sets my world alight
I long to taste every inch of you,
I know you like it the way I do

Your body, a place of endless desire,
Where my heart skips a beat setting my soul on fire
I am not afraid to burn in this wildfire
'Cause you're the only one I admire...!!!

7. SEDUCE

You are my Super Girl
My sweet Wonder Girl
My kinky Spider Girl
My deadly Bat Girl

My sexy Harley Queen
Wearing a super jean
Making me lean
On the skin like a sheen

I don't want to say it
But, I do want to slay it
I don't want to play it
But, I am ready to pay it

You're making me so loose
Like I'm driving a super cruise
I want all of it
So, I am not going to choose

I like your brows
They encourage me a lot
Those twist and turns do tell me
It's worth the shot

I will turn it up to blues
You take off my favourite shoes
You're the master of my heart
Because, of the way you Seduce...

8. COME AND GO!

Days will come and go
This time will come and go
This phase will come and go
Sunrays will come and go

Seasons will come and go
Things will come and go
Years will come and go
All fears will come and go

The tides will come and go
Waves will come and go
These lakes will come and go
Earthquakes will come and go

People will come and go
Friends will come and go
Thoughts will come and go
All feelings will come and go

Clouds will come and go
Doubts will come and go
I'll kill you if you have a doubt!
'Cause, I'm not a passing cloud to come and go

9. WHERE WORDS AREN'T NEEDED

I can still feel your breath on my skin
Warm, lingering, like a quiet promise
Your fingers move slowly,
As if they never want to forget

The night is still, holding us close,
While moonlight spills through the curtains
Your lips trace places on me
That have never known words

Time forgets itself when you're near,
Every second stretching, unravelling,
Lost in the quiet pull of your touch
No rush, it's all about the feeling

15

I know we are not near, but stay. Just like this
Where words aren't needed, where silence is enough,
Where we are more than just bodies
But a language of our own

10. LOVE

What is the thing that sometimes makes you feel
That, you're someone's might?
Also, which makes you realise
That the most beautiful thing in this world is a hug
tight?

Yes, it is the yonder window light
Which in a moment can make you feel all the day and all
the night
Yes, it makes you fight
Even if you're standing on a super scary height

It is a feeling that makes you realise
That, you have a sight
To see this world
with all the colours bright

So, what is the thing?
Which makes you feel super light?
Like a high-flying kite?
You're right...

It is LOVE, the most luscious flight
Taking off in the soft, sweet twilight

11. BEST!

In the season where everyone's so stressed
I don't know why? But, I feel myself lying on your warm
chest
That's my lavishing place from my fantasy world which
is permanently better than any of the remaining rest
The place where I'm resting on is creating a spark of love
which ends up creating our romantic fest

I know life is a test
But, I want to get with your warmth fully dressed
Leaving out signs of my sighs on your crest
This is the magic I yearned for all my life and with
you...now...

I feel so blessed!
You make me progress and never let me rest
And you know what?
My Love, You're the Best!

12. 'CAUSE YOU ARE MINE!

Everything will be fine
Things just need to take their time
Life is just sour like a lime
But, don't worry 'cause you are mine!

I promise to make your journey shine
You're sweet potato and I'm your brine
I will make it last and It's all about time
But, whenever it's you I don't want to wait for even a
rhyme

Don't be stressed, Lets go out for a dine
You can totally take your time
I will take you a place prime
Don't worry 'cause you are mine!

I know life is too hard to climb
Relax, I will be your road sign
And I know you will outshine
'cause you are mine!

Everything will be fine
Things just need to take their time
Life is just sour like a lime
But, don't worry 'cause you are mine!

13. IT RAINS WHEN YOU'RE NOT HERE

It rains when you're not here
It pains when you're not here
My heart veins strain when you're not here
It rains when you're not here!

To me, Rain blames, when you're not here
He's fed up with it always raining, saying this is not fair
I told him this is the last time he's here
Because you're going to be near soon
But I don't know why he is warning and arguing with
me, telling that,
You're never going to be here
You were never my polar bear!

That's scary, I do fear
I need you to hold me tight, close, and near
But until then, he has to rain
'Cause, you're not here!

14. WHEN, MY HAND YOU DID HOLD!

Days are cold
Time is gold
My world turned upside down
When, my hand you did hold!

I was sturdy and bold
Happy but cold
I don't know how I did mould
When, my hand you did hold!

I like it easy and strolled
Leaving all things uncontrolled
After decades, I was paroled
When, my hand you did hold!

I'm unable to withhold
The feelings for you I uphold
It's what my concealed ardour told
That, you're my exquisite diamond and gold

I realised that I want it to be rolled
All things unfold
With you I want to grow old
When, my hand you did hold!

15. GOODBYE!

Life's a bitch,
But, ultimately, it's a ride
A ride that is menacingly threatening, like a scary tide
But now, I don't want to hide

I don't want to lie
Life was good, and then it became dry
I still don't know the answer. Why?
But today is something different.

Something vivid and colourful like a sky
The sky is full of trust, love, and respect only for the
world of mine
Thanks for being my calmness and pride, like a
confidence-enhancing suit with a tie
Thanks for bringing me back alive

With my whole heart happy, warm, and satisfied...!!!
I've never felt this high, in fact
I think I'm the world's luckiest guy
To get a person like you!

Have a lovely day ahead, bub. Goodbye!

16. LOSING

Look! I don't want to write anymore
I don't want to fight anymore
There's some weight on my heart
Hence proved, I'm not a knight anymore

If I want, I can definitely be your Mr. Light
Which will glow your heart and make you smile super
wide
If I want, I can definitely be your Mr. Might
But there will always be a but! And my mind is always
right

I know, I'm not the man you're looking for
I'm really bad at choosing
But I still want to go with it; I love it
I am happy seeing you win, but I can't stop myself from
losing

17. COMPLETE BEING INCOMPLETE

Why about me you're so confused?
Don't do this to me; I feel refused!
I've not done any crime to be accused,
Please don't make me feel that I'm used

Let's start again
Spark again
Be the dim lamp
In the dark again

I'm sure you'll feel the storm
Inside me, which I bring along
In a luscious form,
Putting on our favourite song

I want to feel you
Being a soft rope, I want to reel you
Sum up with you
Unseal you

Yes, I'm a fool
I come again and again. Sing songs for you again and
again
Like others I know, I'm not cool
Now, I have nothing else than my words...
The only left tool...!

I don't want you anymore
I don't know why I ask you to be my core
In the past, you made me feel all complete
But now I feel better because there's no one to cheat
So... I'm complete being incomplete!

18. WELCOME TO LIFE!

Everyone has their own story
Everyone has their own problems
Everyone feels they have suffered a lot
They don't know that, the other person might have gone
through a lot

Everyone will promise you a lot
That they will stay with us and sort
All our problems making our life a beautiful cot
But, when the time comes to be there, they question us
"What?"

Hey, they say everything is going to be fine in the end of
the life
Huhuh! Welcome to life!

19. WHENEVER I WRITE

Whenever I write
My words do fight
In this dark world for the light
To reach a height
to let others see through my sight
To improve humanity with an assurance and not with
the word "might"

Whenever I write
My words do fight
Being your strongest knight
I know that, I am right
and I will continue to write for the bright
Whether it is grey, teal, black, or white

20. IMAGINATION

I like the way when you look into my eyes
I like this closure and you hushing your beautiful sighs
I like when my hands you softly hold
I like you baby cause you are a wonder to behold

But, you are my
You are my
You are my imagination
Imagination
You are my
You are my
You are my imagination
Imagination

They say love is a crime
That's for them pretty fine
I say love is time
The time when you will be mine.

But, you are my
You are my
You are my imagination
Imagination
You are my
You are my
You are my imagination
Imagination

I want you to be in the
Real real real real world of mine
I want you to be in the
Real real real real world of mine...

21. NOWHERE LAND

Welcome to the world of LOVE!

The experience beyond Life and Universe

It will take you to the place named the
NOWHERE LAND

A place which doesn't exist in the reality!